WOMEN LIKE ME

WHISPERS OF THE HEART: TRUE STORIES OF LOVE AND WISDOM

JULIE FAIRHURST

ROCK STAR PUBLISHING

Paperback Edition: ISBN: 978-1-990639-28-9
Interior & Cover Design by STOKE Publishing

Publisher:
Rock Star Publishing British Columbia, Canada
Email: julie@changeyourpath.ca

CONTENTS

Collaborative Publication vii
Disclosure xi
Introduction xv
20 Heartfelt Ways to Share Love and Connection xix

PART 1
WHISPERS OF THE HEART
Theresa Waugh 3
Tracy Dionne 7
Tammie Trites 11
Denise Nickel 17
Anonymous 25
Emily Cronk 31
Brenda Cooper 35
Heather Cullen 43
Lisa Ellis 47
Joanne Smith 53
Loretta Lebreton 59
Patters 63
Linda S Nelson 67
Calli Jensen 73
Angela Runquist 79

PART 2
ABOUT WOMEN LIKE ME
The Women Like Me Community 87
A Place to Belong, A Space to Write, A Movement to Inspire
The Women Like Me Book Series 91
More From Women Like Me 95

Julie Fairhurst 99

"I'm selfish, impatient and a little insecure.
I make mistakes, I am out of control and at times hard to handle.
But if you can't handle me at my worst,
then you sure as hell don't deserve me at my best."

Marilyn Monroe

COLLABORATIVE PUBLICATION

This is a collaborative publication, and you may notice variations in writing style from one piece to another. This is intentional, as it allows each writer to share their story in its authentic voice, preserving the uniqueness of their contribution.

We believe their raw and genuine perspectives bring a richness to this collection that polished writing alone cannot capture. Each story reflects the individual journey and truth of the writer, which we honor and celebrate.

Some of these women are first-time authors, not professional writers, but they have poured their hearts and experiences into these pages.

Every woman participating in the Women Like Me program shares a common purpose: "If my story can help even one person, then sharing it is truly worthwhile."

“Being deeply loved by someone gives you strength while loving someone deeply gives you courage.”

Lao Tzu

DISCLOSURE

Hey there, Dear Reader!

Before you dive headfirst into the captivating stories within the Women Like Me book series, we've got a quick heads-up for you.

While these tales are brimming with inspiration, resilience, and heart, it's important to note that this book is not a substitute for professional medical, psychological, psychiatric, or counseling advice. Yep, you heard us right – we're not here to diagnose or treat any conditions.

Don't get us wrong – we're all about empowering you to embrace your inner warrior and navigate life's challenges with grace and strength. But if any of the stories here hit a little too close to home and you feel triggered or need extra support, know that you are never alone.

Reach out to a trusted friend, family member, or professional who can lend a listening ear, offer a shoulder to lean on, or provide expert guidance. You're never alone in this journey; there's no shame in asking for help when needed.

So flip through these pages, soak up the wisdom, and let these incredible women inspire you to embrace your inner strength. Just remember – lean on your support network and seek the help you deserve when in doubt.

Now, let's embark on this adventure together – with courage, compassion, and a whole lot of heart!

Happy reading!

Women Like Me

"There is never a time or place for true love. It happens accidentally, in a heartbeat, in a single flashing, throbbing moment."

Sarah Dessen

INTRODUCTION

WHISPERS OF THE HEART - TRUE STORIES OF LOVE AND WISDOM

Love, a universal language that binds us all, effortlessly transcends boundaries, cultures, and experiences. It is the golden thread that intricately weaves together the joys of connection, the heartache of loss, and the profound journey toward self-discovery.

This is the central theme in the book Whispers of the Heart—True Stories of Love and Wisdom, in which 16 extraordinary women from the Women Like Me community bare their souls to share deeply personal stories of love, heartbreak, and the transformative power of self-love.

Each story in this collection is as unique as the woman who tells it—each one a vibrant mosaic of life's beauty and challenges. Through their words, readers are transported into moments of romantic passion, the bittersweet lessons of heartbreak, and the unshakable strength that emerges from learning to truly love oneself.

These narratives remind us that we are not alone in our struggles or triumphs and that love—in all its forms—has the power to heal, transform, and elevate. The Women Like Me community is built on the belief that every woman's story matters. By sharing their voices, these 16 women not only honor their own journeys but also inspire others to embrace their truths. With each story, they offer a piece of their heart and invite you to listen closely to your own.

We invite you to immerse yourself in the heartfelt tales within these pages, to laugh, cry, and most importantly, to feel. Let "Whispers of the Heart" remind you of the profound wisdom that comes from love —whether it's love for another, love lost, or the journey of finding love within yourself.

This book is more than just a collection of stories. It is a testament to resilience, an ode to vulnerability, and a celebration of the wisdom that springs from listening to the whispers of the heart. It reminds us that love isn't always about perfection—it's about courage, growth, and the ability to rise again after falling.

As you journey through these pages, you will find inspiration, comfort, and perhaps even a reflection of your own experiences. These stories are beacons, reminding us that we are never alone in our struggles or triumphs. They affirm that love—in all its forms—has the power to heal, transform, and elevate.

The Women Like Me community is built on the belief that every woman's story matters. By sharing their voices, these 16 women not only honor their own journeys but also inspire others to embrace their truths. With each story, they offer a piece of their heart and invite you to listen closely to your own.

We invite you to immerse yourself in the heartfelt tales within these pages, to laugh, cry, and most importantly, to feel. Let Whispers of the Heart remind you of the profound wisdom that comes from love —whether it's love for another, love lost, or the journey of finding love within yourself.

Julie Fairhurst

Founder Women Like Me

"There is nothing I would not do for those who are really my friends. I have no notion of loving people by halves, it is not my nature."

Jane Austen

20 HEARTFELT WAYS TO SHARE LOVE AND CONNECTION

In a world that seems to speed by and keep us apart, it's easy to miss out on those small yet meaningful actions that actually bring us closer together. Love isn't all about the big, showy gestures; it's really about those quiet, everyday moments where we show we care, support, and cherish each other.

The great thing is that showing love doesn't need a fancy occasion or an elaborate plan—just a bit of intention and an open heart.

Here are 20 heartfelt ways to share love and connection, serving as gentle nudges to help us sprinkle more warmth, understanding, and kindness into our relationships, one thoughtful step at a time.

1. **Listen deeply** - Give your full attention, without judgment, when someone shares their thoughts or feelings.

2. **Offer kind words** - Share genuine compliments and encouragement to brighten someone's day.

3. **Help without being asked** - Lend a hand with chores or tasks you know someone might be struggling with.
4. **Be present** - Put away distractions and simply spend quality time together.
5. **Show appreciation** - A heartfelt "thank you" or a note of gratitude can go a long way.
6. **Respect boundaries** - Honor others' needs for space, time, and independence.
7. **Give without expecting** - Offer your help or a small gift, not for recognition, but because you care.
8. **Practice patience** - When disagreements arise, take a breath and choose understanding over frustration.
9. **Share your time** - Check in on loved ones, call an old friend, or visit someone who might feel lonely.
10. **Celebrate each other's wins** - Cheer for their successes, no matter how big or small.
11. **Show physical affection** - A warm hug, a gentle touch, or a friendly pat on the back can convey love without words.
12. **Be encouraging** - Remind someone of their strengths and how far they've come, especially when they're doubting themselves.
13. **Be trustworthy** - Keep their confidence and be someone they can rely on.

14. **Smile often** - A simple, warm smile can lift spirits and show you care.

15. **Be forgiving** - Let go of past grievances and focus on moving forward together.

16. **Share laughter** - Watch a funny movie, tell a joke, or recall a silly memory to create joy and strengthen bonds.

17. **Offer your skills** - Help with something you're good at—whether it's fixing something, cooking, or sharing advice.

18. **Support their passions** - Show interest in what they love, even if it's not your thing, and celebrate their hobbies and dreams.

19. **Show up in times of need** - Be there during difficult moments, offering your presence, support, and understanding.

20. **Love yourself** - By practicing self-love, you can better show love to others, radiating positivity and compassion from within.

We share love with others, but it's also a precious gift to ourselves. When we pause to sprinkle a little kindness, show some patience, or express gratitude, we're really just reinforcing those unseen ties that keep us all linked together.

Think of these 20 ways as simple yet deeply meaningful steps that could trigger waves of connection, happiness, and understanding in our lives. As you try out these acts of love, keep in mind that it's usually the smallest gestures that leave the biggest impression.

By choosing to love with more intention, we have the potential to not only transform our personal relationships but also help create a more compassionate and connected world.

JULIE FAIRHURST

PART 1

WHISPERS OF THE HEART

"If I had to choose between breathing or loving you,
I would say 'I love you'
with my last breath."

Shannon Dermott

THERESA WAUGH

"How you love yourself is how you teach others to love you."
- Rupi Kaur

The Urban Dictionary defines love as "The act of caring and giving to someone else. Having someone's best interest and well-being as a priority in your life. To truly love is a very selfless act."

I'm not sure if I agree with this. I say this because I have been a giver and caretaker most of my life but haven't felt true love. Not once did I feel my family, or a partner prioritized my best interests and well-being.

From birth, I was a burden to my birth mother and father, and their drinking and party life took priority. I was then taken away at the age of four and placed with a family member who would abuse me.

From there, I was adopted by a couple that tried to show me love, but I unfortunately couldn't trust and accept it. Then, getting married at 17, putting my partner and his family first while losing my identity and self-worth from more abuse.

I found true love when I saw my children born and raised. That kept my heart full and fulfilled, but it's different now that they have their own lives. My children have blessed me with grandchildren, whom I love dearly, but something was still missing.

I don't feel love. My heart felt empty as my adult children got busier and needed me less. I am happy they are all independent and have become successful individuals, but I feel lost. I didn't know how to get the love back in my life.

I didn't want another partner. I needed to find love in myself and to love myself and who I was as a person. I needed to discover who I was and what I wanted and needed. I was so busy giving all my love to everyone for years that I didn't know how to love myself.

I have hit menopause as well and didn't know how to deal with the symptoms that you have going through with that. I honestly didn't know my identity. It's been years of trying to put myself first and truly love myself.

I am proud of myself and my accomplishments. I have raised successful children and had a great career, and it's time to celebrate and love me for me. I want to learn more about myself and my family history. Who am I? Where do I come from?

So, I did a DNA test and am learning more about myself. I have committed to finding out more about myself and how I can love myself more each day.

Then, I can give more to others.

Love yourself first, always, and forever.

"When someone loves you, the way they talk about you is different.
You feel safe and comfortable."

Jess C. Scott

TRACY DIONNE

"Love is an anchor; it stops you from drifting away." - Robert Corbert

Love is my Anchor

As a little girl, I always knew love was the way. It was a part of me, I did not know how to be different. Love has been my energy and force through many heartbreaks and breakthroughs.

Love has given me the strength to fight some of life's greatest storms. I look at this gift as my anchor and soul survival in a world full of chaos and pain. It was love that has lifted and guided me in ways I never thought possible. When love is present in a storm in my life, peace, and hope come in, and my soul is lifted.

Love, during life's heartbreak is where the anchoring strength needed to come from, both self-love and others. Heartbreaks in my life where love anchored me through were grief, marriage, divorce, emotional shock, romantic breaks ups, concussion, career, raising two boys, and other life events, just to name a few.

During all the heartbreaks and trials, one value always anchored my soul: "LOVE." I know that love is full of surprises, some good, some bad. However, even the heartbreaks and trials were overpowered by love.

Some lessons were hard to learn when it came to love, especially self-love. Self-love for me really came after my divorce. Marriage was a blessing as I have two beautiful boys out of it. It did not start out with heartbreak and pain, as hopefully no marriage does.

Over the years, my love for life was challenged. Some days, it felt like only a grain of sand of love was left. My family, friends, and school community strengthened my love and kept me anchored in life's storms. The hardest part of loving so deeply is the pain that follows when grief, divorce, and loss hit.

Over the years, I have felt the pain of losing a loved one. It started at age nine when my grandmother passed away suddenly. I remember the tears shed by my mother in the car after school and the quietness in her voice. This was my first memory of experiencing the emotion of grief.

Then, at eighteen years old, I got the most painful call you could ever imagine. My girlfriend Courtney called and said my best friend Nicole was gone. I remember walking from the bedroom to the living room, where my mom and dad were watching television. One looked at me, and they knew something was wrong. I collapsed on the floor sobbing in tears, left speechless. This is the price we pay for love; honestly, I would not change a thing. I have so much gratitude for the friendship and the memories we shared. She passed away suddenly from an illness.

Six months later, my other girlfriend got a phone call saying she had passed from suicide. I was again left to feel the pain of loving someone. It was love that anchored me through the pain.

I also experienced the pain of losing my first romantic relationship. My high school boyfriend and I broke up. My heart was broken at this point, but the anchor of love and my support systems continued to spread love, and I always kept it as one of my strongest values in life.

As I grew older, I added kindness, gratitude, compassion, and empathy to my list of core values to keep anchored during life's storms. I have lost others over the years; another shocking moment was the passing of my girlfriend, Janine, in 2021. We had been friends for over 20 years.

She passed away from cancer. Her story started my writing journey and healing process. I always feel her love around me; honestly, I would not change a thing. Love is funny that way. It guides us to our greatest gifts. The memories we shared of love, joy, and laughter are priceless.

Love is what keeps us strong and builds communities and resilience in our souls. Love has guided me to life's greatest blessings: beautiful romantic relationships, friendships, partners, physical touches, hugs, and kisses. If you truly ask me, this is the gold in life. Love is one of my greatest gifts, and I cherish it.

Love is my anchor in life.

"Love is patient, love is kind. It does not envy, it does not boast, it is not proud. It does not dishonor others, it is not self-seeking, it is not easily angered, it keeps no records of wrongs."

Corinthians 13:4

"Tis better to have loved and lost
than never to have loved at all."

Alfred Lord

TAMMIE TRITES

"In the unexpected moments of life, a single act of kindness can turn strangers into lifelong friends and create bonds that bless generations to come." - Unknown

How To Meet Your Neighbor

While in Surrey, British Columbia, I lived in the only BC Housing complex with my four daughters. I certainly enjoyed living there as the number of friends my girls had was amazing. There were over 100+ townhomes, all with children. Every home had at least two to three children, so as you can imagine, there were always lots of kids in and around my home daily. Most days, my home had a swinging door for kids. I loved it; having so many friends kept my girls busy and out of trouble.

The townhouse next to mine was vacant for a while, and then I was told I had new neighbors with kids about the same age as my youngest. I had never fully seen anyone there much. I had seen the husband a few times, and he was friendly to the point of saying hello when we crossed paths with each other. Then, one day, I saw the wife moving some stuff in but never said hello.

I remember June 19, 2008, like it was yesterday. The day started as usual: getting the kids off to school and me off to work. When I got home, it was the same normal: homework and dinner, letting the kids burn energy, and then off to bed. It was in the early morning, maybe two or three a.m., and suddenly, there was pounding on the door like someone with authority, a police officer. I thought if I just ignored it, they would go away.

Well, now the banging turned into kicking the door. I made my partner at the time get the baseball bat and go to the door. I was still making my way downstairs, wrapping my robe around me. Then my partner said the man was panicking because his wife was having a baby, their cell phone chargers didn't work, and their cordless house phone was missing the batteries; the man kept screaming for me to come and help.

Now, with nothing under my house coat and our cordless phone in hand, I call 911. As I entered their home, I asked where she was, and he pointed to the floor in front of the fridge. As I got in front of her to give 911 an update on the situation, I was like, holy shit, the baby's head out. Well, there is no time like the present to throw my robe between my legs and phone on my shoulder. I bend down, and mom gives a light push, and out comes this little boy.

"Wow," said the 911 operator, "have you delivered children before I don't think I've ever had someone so calm. You should become a maternity nurse; we need people like you."

I didn't want to pull the baby out too far as he still had the umbilical cord and placenta attached; I didn't want to hurt Mom.

As the ambulance arrives, the husband is still in disbelief about what happened. They get the mom and baby boy on the stretcher, and then the husband says to the ambulance staff that they have to wait until I name the baby. I say, " No, no, I can't name him. You don't know me." He says, "You just did this for us, and you should name him."

Having only girls, I was stuck for a name. The only boy's name I could come up with was Cody, my nephew's name. Now the ambulance crew is saying, "Oh my goodness, that is amazing you meet the neighbors in this situation, and they want you to name the baby; you should!".

So, as they were getting ready to leave, I stood beside Mom and said, "Oh, by the way, I'm Tammie, your neighbor, and I think Cody would be a good name for him."

I couldn't sleep, and all I was thinking was, wow, what just happened? I jumped in the shower and just sat there and cried, not because I was sad but because the whole thing was truly a blessing that day.

After I sent the girls to school that day, I went to their house and asked the husband if I could do anything for them. He stated that the kids were still asleep, and he was still running on adrenaline. I offered to clean the kitchen floor for him, as I didn't want the kids to see that and think the worst.

After I returned home, I was just beside myself. After a few hours, I decided to return to their home to ensure Dad was good and to see if he or the kids needed anything. Then this little soft-spoken girl asked me, "Can you take me to see my Mom and baby brother? There was no way I was going to say no! I got her and her brother together, and off to the hospital we went.

When we finally reached her room, the kids were so overwhelmed with the joy of their new little brother. I felt that Mom would change the name, which was okay with me because if I were in her situation, I wouldn't let some strange neighbor name my son.

My nephew's name is Cody Lee Ryan, and the Mom changed her son's name to Ryan Cody. What a full circle this had become. I got to know the entire family when Mom got home, and we have been friends since then.

The Mom had gotten pregnant again and asked me if I would go with her to deliver her next at BC Women's Hospital in Vancouver. And without hesitation, I said, "Yes".

The family was blessed with another girl. When Mom and baby arrived home, Mom called me over and sat me down at the table; I was kind of worried. She then says, "I have something for you, " and places the forms for the baby's birth certificate in front of me. I looked at her with a strange look and asked her, "What does this mean?" She told me to look at the baby's name, and to my surprise, she named her baby girl Emily Tammie after me.

What an absolute honor this was! I have certainly been blessed in more ways than I could ever imagine.

So, get to know your neighbors. I believe we have lost our communities, and we don't know who our neighbors are anymore, and that's sad. Please be kind; give a little wave with a smile and say, Hello". You never know how blessed you can become.

"He's more myself than I am. Whatever our souls are made of, his and mine are the same."

Emily Brontë

DENISE NICKEL

"Life is a journey of remembrance. We are pre-born in love, being loved and received into love eternal." - Denise Nickel

Being Loved: Leaving One to Care for Another

Have you ever felt abandoned or betrayed? Does the world feel unsafe or under-resourced to meet your needs?

This story details actual events, yet the story I told myself about them was untrue. Can you catch how I made these events all about me? Let me take you on the journey eleven years ago that resolved my feelings of abandonment and betrayal.

The title of this chapter was "Betrayal: Leaving One to Care for Another" until I started writing it. Now, my soul knows a better, higher perspective. I have always been deeply loved and so have you.

Your journey of being loved is just that, being loved. Always and in all ways. I have never been betrayed, neither have you.

October 27, 2014

Lying poolside at an all-inclusive resort in Mexico, I cried as I recalled the heartbreak of bringing home our newborn daughter and having to juggle the attention given to my firstborn.

Why does this memory so trigger me? Why do I want to fight or flee? Why am I still crying over this nine years after it happened?

October 17, 2014

I haven't had a drink of Fireball in five weeks. My drinking was hidden. I only dared drink what my husband brought home. It wasn't the volume. It was an insatiable need. I was a mess.

The direction was clear: Go to Alcoholics Anonymous and find a sponsor. A sponsor found me. She was a nurturing mother. I felt like a little girl. She fed me soup and covered me with blankets of love.

I was her one-and-only. Or so I thought.

Without warning, I met her at Denny's, and we weren't alone. She had two other sponsees. I saw RED and fled the restaurant, shaken to my core.

May 19, 2001

Just keep walking.

Walking and praying. It was one way to rise above my sense of betrayal.

My only comfort was remembering Jesus said, “Forgive them, Father, for they don’t know what they are doing.” He knew how betrayal felt and rose above His circumstances.

My Dad was getting married, and I made it all about me. My stepmom had died a few months earlier, so I thought he would finally have time for me.

Now, another woman stepped in, and I was devastated.

June 10, 1994

This was the memory I couldn't shake. When I needed to feel bad for myself, my mind landed here, like a spot in a well-worn carpet.

I told my sweet 18-month-old child he was a "Big Boy" now. After a C-section, I couldn't lift him when he reached up for me.

I was needed elsewhere. His sister was five weeks old. I was sleep-deprived and sore. I was no longer his all-in-all. I was heartbroken for years.

1966

This is a wisp of a memory – a fleeting thought anchored in the memories of others.

My dad led my three-year-old twin sister and me to our bunk beds for a nap and said goodbye. My sister, Sue, at four and a half, remembered walking with him to the candy store. My brother, at five, had a photographic memory.

My dad returned to see if reconciliation with our mother was possible after their divorce. He had a new family in Washington state, so he needed to know for sure.

I didn't see him again for another 10 years.

During the years of my having and raising small children, I lived within the pages of a book called Can You Hear Me: Tuning in to the God Who Speaks by Brad Jersak.

Whenever I was upset or had a troubling memory, I would ask Jesus, "Where were you when this happened?" I invited Jesus to return with me so I could relive memories from a heavenly perspective and find solace in my emotional pain.

So, I was crying poolside in October 2014, feeling sorry for myself and my firstborn, imagining that we were both somehow damaged because our bond was broken.

Later, I returned to my room, grabbed a pen and paper, and asked Jesus, "Why does this still hurt?" In my spiritual ears, I heard, "Let me show you." Then, Christ took me to the day of my birth.

August 29, 1963

4:47 AM

I sensed myself in an incubator. I am cold and crying, and the lights are so bright!

I struggled to breathe, using every abdominal muscle I had to get enough air into my six-week premature lungs.

I had the doctor's and nurse's full attention for 20 minutes.

Then everyone left me!

They realized this was a multiple birth!

5:07 AM

My identical twin sister was caught behind our mother's ribs. She was bruised, smaller, and in need of rescue.

When my mom was told she had twins, she said, "You're shittin' me!" That's my mom!

They were expecting one boy, Daniel Glen, but now were the proud parents of two little girls, Denise and Danelle.

In my vision with Jesus, all attention was suddenly on Danelle. They left me to care for another. This is where my psyche was first exposed to abandonment, betrayal, and lack.

Suddenly, I saw Jesus bending over the incubator. His robed arm shielded me from the light and the frigid air. Then, He put His mouth on mine and gave me breath.

Inhale. Exhale. Inhale. Exhale.

I spent weeks in the hospital, my sister even longer. I was always told we were born with "holes in our chests."

Once I experienced Jesus' presence at my birth, I understood I had never been alone. Through the years, my faith and understanding have deepened and broadened.

In A.A., I was encouraged to find a God of my understanding. I couldn't get it wrong if I found a loving, accepting, supportive, and peaceful Presence.

In The Work of Byron Katie, she asks, "What is the turnaround?" The "turnaround" reverses beliefs to reveal new perspectives.

How have I betrayed myself in each of these instances?

I judged others and myself as unloving when I could not know that was true. My unmet expectations led to my inner conflict and suffering.

What does this all mean, and what does this mean for you?

Why did I write this chapter?

I want you to know that you can know the unknowable while on the planet. Insight is available just for asking. Prayer is listening.

You will know pain on your journey of being loved. Yet, the Presence of Love meets any perceived violation of trust or confidence.

Being loved is our journey, always and in every way.

Love is like water; it is constantly flowing, always available, and will not stop. But you must be ready to receive it and let it flow through you.

When you feel betrayed, recall your most loving memory. Let it surround you, breathe it in, and let it fill your heart. Lift your perspective. Life is love in full expression.

Leaving one to care for another is a human perspective.

I know better now, and I hope you do too.

You are so very loved.

"If you find someone you love in your life, then hang on to that love."

Princess Diana

ANONYMOUS

"The weak can never forgive.
Forgiveness is an attribute of the strong." - Gandhi

Unconditional love takes many different forms. I have a secret, and I don't know how else to tell it but to do it here. I've been in a 20-year relationship with a neurodiverse alcoholic. We've been married for nearly 14 years, and it's come with many ups and downs. It also comes with two beautifully unique neurodiverse children that I love unconditionally.

Unconditional love has many different forms. It can look like mothering a child that was highly colicky for months and didn't sleep well for three years, that exhausted you beyond all levels imaginable, but you continue to care for them and love them with everything you've got and more!

That child grows up to have ADHD, sensory processing disorder, and OCD, and they cause you to burn out all the time, but you learn how to take care of yourself better than ever before, so you can continue to give your love no matter what.

You learn to meditate and ask source to heal, replenish, and recharge your energy so you can be love to this amazing little soul. You co-regulate them because they can't calm their emotions themselves. You seek natural healing options rather than deeming them sick and medicating them. You get them hypnotherapy, access bars, reiki, sound baths, chiropractic treatments, and whatever is needed to support them.

Unconditional love can look like mothering a child who claims she's a furry and a therian, and you allow this child to behave in ways many don't deem normal, and you love and support her along the way.

You allow them to buy masks and tails and make fun videos with them. Later on, they realize they identify as LGBTQ and announce they are gay. You love and support them again without hesitation. Next thing you know, they announce they are nonbinary and would like to change their name. You inform the school that your kid would like to be referred to by a different name and ask the school to support this so your child's mental health will be less fragile.

You ensure your child can be involved in Pride events, LGBTQ clubs, and therapy so they have the tools and resources to grow healthy and safe. You assure this child that you have their back and will always love them no matter what they throw at you.

Unconditional love can look like forgiveness of infidelity, drug and alcohol abuse, and a relationship that has been full of dishonesty. It can look like healing yourself while still in the relationship. It can be letting go of resentment and learning to trust again. It can look like learning each other's love languages and taking couples counseling. It can be loving this person despite all that went wrong and giving your relationship a fighting chance. It's an effort where many people would just give up.

Unconditional love can look like getting a job after 11 years of being a full-time stay-at-home mom and a self-employed entrepreneur. It's seeing that your dollars earned need to increase, and it's taking the steps to contribute more financially to your family when it's needed.

Unconditional love is unpredictable and can sneak up on you when you're not looking for it. It can be working 20 hours a week at your new job and noticing something strange is happening. After only a few short weeks, you begin to notice your heart beats harder around someone new, and you can't get this person out of your head day or night.

You notice you find all their little mannerisms, quirks, and expressions endearing, and you enjoy every second of every day you're with them. You notice they make you smile all the time and laugh so easily. You notice how much they build you up and inspire you to be better. You notice you feel adored, admired, desired, and loved in a way you have never seen before.

You begin to suspect you are in love, but you don't even know what falling in love looks like anymore because you did that 20 years ago. You start searching online for 'signs you are falling in love,' and a few articles confirm it. You are, in fact, in love with your boss, and he's old enough to be your father.

You've been able to look at this person for the soul he is and see no age gap. Despite their signs of aging, you can see that they are still very much full of life, vitality, strength, wisdom, maturity, and passion. They possess all of the qualities you would be looking for in a partnership if you were looking, but you're not.

You weren't even open to falling in love, yet it still happened. You can't help but hug this person every time you see them, and you can't help but feel a euphoric high when you are close. Your oxytocin and dopamine levels are off the charts, and the interconnectedness of your souls is mind-blowing. You feel such a strong pull in this new direction and are now conflicted.

You've been giving your marriage everything you've got, yet it still feels stale or without passion. Everything that's been missing for years is there in front of you, waiting for you to claim it. You don't want to cause your husband heartbreak, but you also don't want to break the heart of your soulmate. You notice your own heart feels full for the first time ever, but you have kids to consider in any decision you make.

You've weighed out many ideas in your head of how life looks moving forward, and still, everything is unknown. You've considered an open marriage, and you've considered divorce.

You've even considered falling deeper in love and keeping it a secret, but you've realized you can't hold in this secret any longer. The truth must be set free, so you write about it and release it to the universe to handle.

Now that my story is out... it's time for a new chapter.

"Never love anyone who treats you like you're ordinary."

Oscar Wilde

EMILY CRONK

"When someone you love becomes a memory,
the memory becomes a treasure." - Unknown

Love Bug

In your eyes, my soul found home,
we shared one breath; I was not alone,
we were intertwined together yet betwixt,
what I'd give for a century lost in that bliss.

The first night,
stars adorned the sky,
crescent moon hung low,
our hearts beating high.

Hunger for affection,
our love did ignite,
you were swimming in my veins
a desire so bright.

But now, you're lost in thought,
your soul astray,
where the willow's branches whisper,
"fade away."

I thought our magic,
would forever bind,
your body lost,
within the forest of time.

As evening comes,
hear my song,
a melancholy tide,
I love you deeply.

But tonight,
I felt your magic die,
you've gone with the sun,
this the final pain.

When you leave,
leave me with one memory to sustain,
let me recall that afternoon,
sun shining bright on your face,

"I love you too" you exclaimed,
that feeling, you cannot replace.
Dylan, my sweet bug, so true.

I'll remember your love,
when your lost,
and I'm left missing you.

"Love is needing someone. Love is putting up with someone's bad qualities because they somehow complete you."

Sarah Dessen

BRENDA COOPER

"Life Is Better With A Dog" - Unknown

It's a Dog's Life

Dogs have filled my life with their unwavering companionship from my childhood to the understanding of adulthood. Their presence has brought joy, comfort, and meaning to every chapter of my journey. These cherished fur children, as I lovingly call them, have not only shared my life but shaped it, leaving a tender, everlasting imprint on my heart.

My heart has echoed with the quiet whispers of love and loss, the kind only a dog can bring into your life. I've experienced the joy of their companionship and the deep sorrow of their absence. And through it all, the wisdom they leave behind is a quiet, steadfast presence—reminding me daily of the responsibility, love, and emotional bond that defines our time together.

Each of them had their story, their unique way of embedding themselves in my soul. Some had come to me as tiny, uncertain bundles, wide-eyed and full of wonder. Others had found their way into my life with scars both seen and unseen, their trust a gift earned over time. They all taught me about love, patience, and the delicate art of listening—not with my ears but with my heart.

Although there were many beloved fur children in my life, I will begin this journey with our Cooper boy, an American Staffy, who was the first dog to join our blended family. He was a tiny blur of energy and mischief, his eyes a mirror of boundless joy. Cooper was a soul with eyes that saw straight through to my heart. I met him at the SPCA, where I used to go on my lunch break. He was one of eight puppies in a kennel, and he stole my heart. I desperately wanted to bring him home, but unfortunately, it did not seem to be possible.

One day, while I was at work, my young daughter came through the doors, huffing and puffing, calling my name. As I looked over the counter, I saw her struggling with all her strength to hold this puppy. I burst into tears as my husband and my son followed behind her; my husband had gone to the SPCA and adopted him.

Cooper joined our family, fulfilling our destiny to be together. He taught all of us responsibility—the early mornings, the late nights, the sacrifices willingly made for the promise of his wagging tail. He showed me that love was not just a feeling but an action, a commitment to care. He was with us for an amazing 14 years until his old age took him from us.

I was devastated. The despair of his absence felt like an endless storm, yet within the heartbreak, there was wisdom. The space he had filled with his loyalty and playfulness was now hollow, and the devastation and grief of his passing left a profound ache in my chest. Yet, even as he departed, Cooper's love remained in every corner of my home, tucked in the folds of memory. He taught me that loving a dog means being open to both the joy of their companionship and the heartbreak when their time with us is done. I have a tattoo of Cooper's paw prints on my arm, and he is with me every day. Missed always my Poopy Coopy.

Not long after Cooper, Gunner entered our lives; he was so special and helped fill that huge hole in my heart. He brought a new kind of love; he was such a beautiful pup and was so adorable and funny. As he grew, he was such a proud boy. He was a strong and noble English Staffy. He had the biggest smile, and he knew it; his gentle and kind personality won the hearts of many. It is funny how we have nicknames for our fur children, and he was my Gunner Bunner. We had a heartfelt bond forged through years of shared moments.

When we moved to the farm in 2021, he was eight years of age. I hoped the wide-open spaces would be a blessing for him, but on a cold New Year's Day in 2023, he left us at almost ten years of age and passed away in my lap. I was filled with anger and guilt for not recognizing his illness sooner; he was so resilient and determined that he never displayed any symptoms. By the time we realized something was wrong, all we could do was keep him comfortable.

The grief was sharp; it ripped me apart, and in that moment, I realized it was about knowing that someday we would be the ones left behind, holding their love in our hearts. It took me two days before I could even speak to my children, let alone any of our friends. This year, I plan to tattoo the prints of his paws on my arm next to my beloved Cooper.

During Gunner's time, crazy dog lady me fell in love with the Staffy breed, and we welcomed two more Staffies into our hearts, Zoey and Odin, who are aunt and nephew. Zoey, our queen, who makes sure you know she is the queen with all her verbal requests daily. I call her my old lady now, as she is nine years old this year and loves her freedom on the farm, helping Dad with the chores and keeping him company.

And then there is Odin; he is our nutter. His countless crazy antics keep you laughing, and his obsession with balls, sticks, twigs, and literally anything he can find—even if it is as small as a pinhead—he will bring it to you to throw and will hound you until you do. He is my special boy, and yes, he is definitely a mama's boy.

Zoey, my sweet Staffy queen, is turning ten this year. She's grown older, but her heart is still as vibrant as it ever was. As she ages and I look upon her adorable grey face, I see in her the same grace that all my dogs have shown over the years—the quiet wisdom of a creature who has lived fully, loved deeply, and given all that she has without hesitation.

Moving to the farm and having livestock naturally necessitated the need for a livestock dog, but I could not settle for just one; I had to have three. Pyrrha, our beautiful and loving mom, who considers herself a 120-pound lap dog and enjoys cuddling with me on the couch, gets very jealous of the baby lambs during lambing season. Pyrrha is rude to the ewes and thinks they're her babies, so we don't let her in the paddocks until they're weaned.

After suffering abuse as a young dog, Titan, our gentle giant, unexpectedly came to us. His timid and scared face captured our hearts, prompting us to immediately rescue him. He is the most exceptional and steadfast livestock dog ever; everyone adores him and consistently expresses their desire to adopt him immediately. Of course, that would never happen, as he holds a special place in our hearts.

Then there is their daughter Freya, who follows in Dad's footsteps and is gentle and kind. However, she can also be protective, alerting us to anything that is not right on the property. Despite the fact that farm dogs are supposed to be outdoors 24 hours a day, my heart couldn't tolerate leaving them outside at night. They sleep inside in our back room, where they are still close to the barns. Each of them brought their own flavor of love to the house. Pyrrha is strong and steady, Titan is gentle and wise, and Freya—her energy, her brightness—reminded me every day of the joy that dogs can bring.

Someone approached us one day, asking if we would be interested in adopting a beautiful white pup. I drove out to meet him and fell in love immediately. A week later, we adopted Echo, our beautiful, funny, silly Aussie shepherd. He came to us deaf, and we loved him so much. He was the sweetest boy. His blue eyes were so gentle and loving.

We taught him sign language, and he wore a collar that vibrated to bring him back when he was outside. He loved to run outside on the farm in all the glorious space. He would engage in the most bizarre activities, such as chasing sunlight across the floor and licking cupboard doors. His antics would leave me shaking my head in laughter. We lost him one spring day, when he was about two years old.

That day left a profound void in my heart; it was a devastating and tragic accident, and I am at a loss for words as I have never lost a fur child in such a tragic way. We gently laid him to rest on the farm, atop a beautiful small hill at the end of my garden, with a spectacular view and a marker visible from the house. I look out for him every morning.

Through all these years, one thing has become clear to me: dogs teach us more about life than we could ever imagine. They show us how to love without conditions, to care for others with an open heart, and to be present in every moment. They teach us that the joy of a wagging tail or a soft nuzzle can heal even the deepest wounds, and that the pain of their passing is the price we pay for their love.

No matter how many dogs come into my life or how many I lose, the love they leave behind will always be with me. They teach me that healing doesn't mean forgetting; it means carrying forward the love that never fades.

As I sit quietly, surrounded by my fur children, I feel the whispers of those who are no longer here. Their voices are soft but steady, an unbroken melody of love and wisdom. They remind me that though their physical presence is gone, their spirits are eternal, alive in my memories and the lessons they've left behind.

In their love, I have found my purpose. In their absence, I have found my strength. And in their whispers, I have found my heart. The house was quiet in the stillness of dawn, save for the faint sound of nails clicking on the floor. Those soft steps were a comforting rhythm, a reminder that love surrounded me in the simplest of moments. My heart swelled, as it always did, at the sight of them—my dogs, my companions, my family.

“I have decided to stick to love...Hate is too great a burden to bear.”

Martin Luther King Jr

HEATHER CULLEN

"Try to be a rainbow in someone's cloud." - Maya Angelou

I guess I should start by saying that I never expected my life to take the path it has taken.

When I was a young girl in the Kootenays in British Columbia, I grew up with a single and divorced mother, and of course, that was not what most kids had back then. I dreamed of a white picket fence and all that came with it. Unfortunately, or should I say, fortunately, that was not to be my path.

My mother worked on dam sites, so we moved a lot. She was single, so she had lots of friends and taught me to dance to my own beat and never follow anyone blindly. She also gave away two other children, who my sister and I didn't know about until we were in our 30s, but that is another story.

Mostly, what she taught me was to love unconditionally.

This most likely led to me having been blessed to have four boys. They have three different fathers and each but one was a good dad and husband. Each died, and I spent years being a caretaker to them all.

My story is about how we can take such loss and become better and stronger and have the heart begin to heal from it. I have passed on my love and care to the four amazing boys I have raised, who are kind, gentle, and loving men.

The heart is capable of loving so many in our lives for each gift they give us, and the hardest lesson to learn is how to let go with love.

The more love you feel, the harder the grief will be when they are gone, and that is not an easy path to take.

I have also lost my dad (cancer), mom (cancer), sister (drugs), and many friends. Each one has a special place in my heart that will never truly heal, but I will continue to love and share my heart, but it's not easy.

I find it hard sometimes to open my heart again to new chances to meet and love others. Sometimes, my heart is so full of pain. At times, from the memories of those who have left, I am not sure if I can continue to love without reservation like I did when I was younger.

Like everyone, I cling to my relationships with people who are still here, and sometimes, I miss out on new opportunities to meet and love more people.

"This is a good sign, having a broken heart. It means we have tried for something."

Elizabeth Gilbert

LISA ELLIS

"Everyone has a story to tell, a lesson to teach, and wisdom to share... Life is a beautiful masterpiece bound together by your experience. Open up and share your story; become an inspiration to others. You can make a difference because you matter. You were created with purpose. Live your life with intention, go out there and make a difference by being the difference." - Melanie Koulouris

"Your Mom has Cancer!"

The year 2022 was the worst year of my life. When I say year, I mean pretty much the whole year.

In January, when the year started, we were hoping for a good year, just like everybody else, wishing everyone a "Happy New Year" of good health and well blessings. Little did we know that was short-lived when my Mom got diagnosed with Lung cancer at the beginning of March of that year.

It all started with a lump on her shoulder. "Hey Lisa, " she said, one day when I was speaking to her on the phone, which we did often, every day, sometimes multiple times a day, as I have always had a close relationship with my Mom. "I have this lump on my shoulder, and it just doesn't look right. I think I am going to get it checked," she told me. "That's a good idea, Mom," I replied.

So she made an appointment with our family Doctor. He said, "It's a cyst, Linda. I can remove it for you and send it to be tested." She confirmed with the Doctor to go ahead with the procedure.

March 4, the year of 2022, started out as a normal day, just like any other. I had just finished making my morning coffee when the phone rang. It was my Mom and little did I know that this call would change my life forever.

When I answered, my Mom told me that the Doctor's office had called her and wanted her to see him immediately regarding her test results. "That's odd that he would want to see me unless something showed," she said. "It's okay Mom. Try not to worry too much until you know for sure. It might not be anything," even though I felt that wasn't the case. "You're right, Lisa. Thank you," she said before we hung up the phone.

I asked her if she wanted me to go with her, but she said my stepfather would be with her. Despite her fears, Mom went to her appointment at 5:30 in the evening. I called her that evening from work to see how her appointment went; when my stepfather answered, he confirmed my fears. I can still hear the panic or disbelief in his voice as he gave me the terrifying news, "Honey, I'm sorry to tell you that your Mom has Cancer!" he said. It's a floater that came from somewhere else in her body, so they are going to test her lungs, brain, and bones because he said that lungs and brain usually go hand in hand." Your Mom is praying with the ladies right now. She will call you back."

Devastation just hit me. When I hung up the phone, I cried so hard, harder than I have ever cried before. I remember thinking, how could this be true? I prayed every day, numerous times a day. I don't want my Mom to die. But guess what? I didn't have a choice. I could do nothing but be there for my Mom in any way I could.

My Mom called me back a few moments later, but I didn't even know what to say. All I could say at that moment was, "I am sorry you are sick, Mom. I am here for you."

We found out later, after further testing, that she had Stage 4 terminal Lung Cancer, for which there was no cure. My Mom was set up with VON Sakura House to have a Nurse go and do weekly checkups on her.

They started her on oxygen right away because, on the Nurse's first visit, Mom's oxygen was low. The Nurses were great. After Mom's Cancer diagnosis, I was sitting in her lobby with her one day, and she asked me if I could make a stand for Cancer. She knew that I was publishing a book about MS (Multiple Sclerosis), which I did publish before Mom's passing. She looked at me and said, " Lisa, maybe you can write a book about Cancer someday?!" I looked at her and replied, "Maybe." "Tell people everything they need to know."

I have watched my Mom slowly lose her independence. I have watched her getting weaker and weaker. I have watched her taking pill after pill, having a Nurse visit after Nurse visit. I have watched my Mom struggling to breathe, and I have heard her cough and cough, and there would be times when she couldn't even speak. I sat with her as she cried and tried to comfort her as we both cried together as she spoke about her dying wishes.

I was there with her the day she became so weak, and within an instant, I was there to grab her as she said, "Lisa, grab me, I am going to fall." Sadly, my Mom lost her battle with Lung Cancer the next day, July 11, 2022, just four months after being diagnosed.

So, I have decided to honor my Mom and carry on her legacy as she lives on through me. I plan to do what I can to have my Mom's memory live on in hopes that I can offer valuable information, comfort, hope, support, and strength to others who are facing terminal illnesses of their own.

Just two months after I lost my Mom to Lung Cancer, my sister was diagnosed with Stage 4 Cancer of the Pancreas and sadly, she passed six months after being diagnosed. So I lost my Sister on March 20, 2023, just eight months after I lost my Mom. She was just 44. They are the two strongest people I know, and through them, I have gained strength.

Despite their struggles, they both fought a hard fight. As hard as it was, I am so thankful that I was there with both of them during their battle, during their emotional meltdowns, during the confusion and the chaos, during the uncertainty, standing strong for them, and with them up until they both took their last breath.

I had to make sure they were okay, that they weren't alone, and that I reassured them that they were strong, beautiful, and loved as a reminder that I was there for them and with them, no matter what. They were the center of my life, and I will continue to honor them for the rest of mine.

You don't even know the effects Cancer has on a family until it happens to you!

"What's meant to be will always find a way."

Trisha Yearwood

JOANNE SMITH

"Dogs are not our whole life,
but they make our lives whole." - Roger Caras

Georgie and Me

There is something to be said about that secure feeling you have with your spouse of 16 years. Knowing you won't grow old alone, you'll always have each other's backs, and all the traveling you have planned for in your retirement is nearing.

A second marriage that overshadows all the learning curves of the first. Awww, how bliss. We made it! Of course, no blessing is without hiccups. The hiccups tell us how strong we are as a couple.

My spouse and I supported each other emotionally through the deaths of three of our parents; we grew a successful business together and rode the agonizing roller coaster of my son's struggle with alcoholism, substance abuse, and homelessness.

Unbeknownst to me, no one could have prepared me for what eventually shattered my sense of security with this man. For $240 an hour, twice a month, he found another way to relieve the stress associated with the trials and tribulations of being a supportive husband. Her name was Mari.

The next four years of my life were spent in therapy. The first two years were spent thinking our marriage was strong enough to survive this indiscretion. Unfortunately, it was not; I was unable to forgive him. My anxiety was extremely high after having lived in this state of disarray and indecision for two years. Its disabling effect found me with long periods of isolation and depression.

I did not leave the house unless I had a therapy or doctor's appointment. My world was shattered and I had difficulty interacting with others and within my surrounding environment.

As a child and young adult, I survived physical, emotional, and sexual abuse. Nonetheless, I had no idea how crushing this intense feeling of loneliness and betrayal could be. During these first two years, I had inquired about getting a service dog. My therapist and I had discussed the benefits...having something positive to focus on, enabling my social exposure, and calming my now PTSD symptoms.

I spent some time researching and found an organization that trained and certified the dog for you. The cost: $20,000.00!! At the time, I found no other options available, so I agreed to the terms. Most trainers and organizations who trained service dogs worked with large breeds. I was, and still am, struggling to manage chronic pain from a degenerative back injury in my 30's. I wanted a small breed, and this organization assured me they would find me a small dog.

Eventually, they came up with a 40 lb Corgi. I was hoping for something smaller, but I thought I would give the 14-day trial period a try. Tucker was a beautiful dog, well-trained in public, and had a calming demeanor. There was only one problem. He took off after squirrels while on and off leash, often twisting and pulling on my back as he jerked forward.

Unfortunately, I was not able to manage this aspect of his behavior and, with a heavy heart, returned him to his trainer. We tried two other dogs after that, but with no success. I had given up hope of ever finding a suitable service dog.

At this point in my life, I continued therapy and signed a separation agreement with my husband. Discovering my strengths through therapy and learning to manage a large house alone proved challenging.

Into the first year of the separation, my ex decided to get a dog, a very rambunctious but endearing little 15 lb Jack Russell Terrier. He was a rescue dog with anxiety and trust issues (hmmm, sounds familiar). I questioned my ex's decision to take on the responsibility of a dog because our business required him to be on the road a lot, and he traveled often.

At first, my ex got me to look after this dog one to two days a week while he managed certain aspects of our business. However, once he started traveling again, I had to take this little dog seven to ten days at a time. Of course, we started to bond.

Georgie began to hide behind me when my ex came to pick him up. Soon, he stopped eating when with my ex and whined constantly. My ex decided it was best if the dog stayed with me...I agreed! After researching training your own service dog, I found a lady who trains all dogs...aggressive, behavioral, basic training, and service dogs. Although she had never taken on the vivacious personality of a Jack Russel Terrier, she felt that after talking to me on the phone for an hour, I would be invested enough to take on the task.

Grace, the trainer, came to my house every two weeks for two hours for about six months. It cost me only a fraction of what other businesses quoted me. We then started taking Georgie's training into the public... grocery stores, the pet store, and the mall. He was fully trained in eight months. He sits when I stop walking and looks to me for instruction. He is trained to wait at the bottom or top of the stairs and proceed only when instructed to do so. This prevents possible falls on the stairs, which is a caution due to my back injury. He is trained to approach me if I am having a PTSD moment and calm me.

In public, when I find I am most anxious, he keeps me focused ... making sure he is safe and out of danger of shopping carts, not in anyone's way, and is near enough to me to provide service. At first, the constant attention he drew in public was difficult for me to manage. The last thing I want is to draw attention to myself. I just want to get in and get out, unseen.

However, everyone wants to talk to me about Georgie. They want to know his breed, what kind of service dog he is, and to tell me how cute he is. And even though his service dog vest says 'do not pet,' they want to pet him. Certainly, an obstacle I faced with Georgie in Public.

Now, I am more comfortable and have learned some tactics to avoid this unwanted attention from people. I try not to make eye contact, and I put my hand between the person reaching out and Georgie if they try to initiate contact. Georgie has become the center of my life because he has given me my life back.

I now attend a gym three days a week and have joined a walking club and writers group meeting. I meet friends in town for lunch and go shopping by myself ...with Georgie. I have met new friends along the way, and I am enjoying being back in the game.

I love this little dog so much. He is with me 24/7. I believe we are more connected than most human beings. I thought my traveling days were over, but we flew out to Alberta together last fall, and we are heading to Aruba to visit a friend for two weeks this coming March/25.

Georgie and I have healed each other, making us both complete.

"Two people in love, alone, isolated from the world, that's beautiful."

Milan Kundera

LORETTA LEBRETON

"You have to learn to love yourself before you can love someone else. Because it's only when we love ourselves that we feel worthy of someone else's love." - Alyssa B. Sheinmel

It was October, and I was offered an opportunity to go to Victoria, British Columbia, to work for seven weeks. The situation wasn't ideal, but the opportunity was a great one.

I was scared and nervous because I'd never been to Victoria. I also have never been away from home for that length of time. Over the last few years, I have gone through so much in my personal life trying to learn to love myself. And I decided that this could be a great thing for me.

Everything fell into place. I was able to secure a place to stay. That was very close to my work and close to the downtown. My job kept me busy during the day. But the weekends remind me to do whatever I choose.

I'd never had that, and I was going to take advantage of this time. To truly find myself and to find self-love. I've worked through so much. But really learning to love myself and to enjoy spending time with myself. It was something I hadn't done. I feel like maybe I was afraid to be alone with me.

I decided on my first weekend there, that I would go to a restaurant by myself. This ended up being a bit more challenging than expected. I went to a couple of restaurants. But I got nervous and walked out.

I found a nice restaurant. I went inside, sat down, and enjoyed a nice meal. And enjoyed being alone with me. It was a different feeling and a little uncomfortable at first. But once I accomplished that, it became easy to continue doing it while I was there. I went for more dinners alone and for walks through beautiful parks. On a self-guided tour through a Castle. I went on guided tours through the city. I want to an art gallery on my own. I did so much while I was there. But the best thing I ever did was spend this time with me.

I did do some things with co-workers as well. But the most important was getting to know me. I came home feeling so empowered and so much love for me. I had lost myself in a toxic relationship 15 years ago and was so afraid to let go of that connection that I had with him. We had separated four years ago, but I kept trying to fix what was broken and always ended up in the same spot—feeling unloved and shattered. I finally realized that I had allowed the relationship to destroy the carefree, fun-loving person. I was. I've spent the last four years trying to find that person again, but I still had the fear of not having him in my life. I couldn't just let go.

I ended the connection to that relationship and have started spending more time with myself. I have taken a larger look at my future and where I see myself. I'm proud of my progress from being in Victoria.

One of the people I met there told me that no matter how many times I read a book, the ending was still the same. He was right. That chapter of my life was never going to change, no matter how hard I tried.

I am writing a new chapter now. This is a beautiful one full of laughter and love. I have found that beautiful woman who was lost for so long, and I have started loving her in a way that no one ever has.

"For the two of us, home isn't a place. It is a person. And we are finally home."

Stephanie Perkins

PATTERS

"Angels are the messengers of hope, delivering messages of encouragement and reminding us to never give up."
- Gabrielle Bernstein

A Whispered Message From Heaven

She whispered a message to me that night...

"Have no fear, my darling daughter. I'm always near. It's not your time; please stay right here. Live your life with purpose despite the struggles you may encounter. I'll be by your side throughout the rest of your journey; just watch for my signs.

I woke up feeling a sense of calm from the anxiety I had had for months following her passing. Was it a dream, a hallucination, or did my mom whisper gentle words of love from heaven to remind me to keep going forward? I believe that they were gentle whispers!

I've always believed in spirit and sometimes felt the presence of loved ones who passed, but this time, it was different. Dream or not, this time, I was blessed with a much-needed message from my special angel in heaven. I needed to keep going and never give up.

My mom passed in September 2023 at the age of 90 with me at her bedside. It was the hardest thing I've had to do, but I knew I needed to let her go and give her permission to leave my side. Mom and I had a special bond; she was my best friend.

I was born with Spina Bifida, a neural tube defect, and from that moment on, Mom wrapped me in her loving arms and gave me the strength to be brave throughout the obstacles that I was going to face in life. Raising a child with a disability was no easy feat.

From the very beginning, the decisions my parents had to make were unimaginable. I was the fourth child out of five daughters and aside from the demands of parenting and operating their own business, my Mom especially went through many hurdles being my primary caregiver.

From the repeated decision-making regarding whether to proceed with surgeries, long hospital stays, doctors and specialist visits, and continual physical therapy, my Mom found the courage to support me through each of them.

When I was a young girl, I tried to end my life as I had difficulty dealing with my disability and being so different from my childhood peers. I had blocked this out of my memory until I was in my late teens, and Mom wrapped me in her arms once again and told me to keep moving forward no matter what may happen.

Even as an adult, Mom continued to provide her love and supportive encouragement as I made my way through the many obstacles that life presented. Losing loved ones is one of the most heart-wrenching experiences that we all go through at some point in our lives, and the many emotions that grief brings are tremendous. I've lost many of my loved ones throughout my lifetime, and with each passing, it's been an emotional rollercoaster.

I struggled with the passing of my husband, my father, and many other family members and friends. I'm sure many people can relate to these emotions of numbness, anger, guilt, depression, sadness, fear, and anxiety that come with grief. No matter how the person passes, whether it is from age, illness, disability, self-infliction, accidents, fire, homicide, or other tragedy or trauma, it sends us into shock and the realization that our loved one is no longer with us in the physical form.

It seems that grief lingers on throughout our lifetime; however, the intensity of the loss lessons with time and is different for everyone. I believe that we receive signs from our lost loved ones in different forms. It might be finding a feather or dime in a random place, a visit from a specific bird like a dove, blue jay, or cardinal, a memorable song, repetitive angel numbers, a rainbow, or a meaningful message.

Receiving these signs and messages helps us to remember our loved ones and provides us with emotional guidance to carry on, knowing that they are with us in spirit, always watching over us.

I acknowledge that many people don't believe in signs from heavenly angels, which is perfectly okay as it is their belief. Yet I know in my heart that what I've experienced and often encounter from many of these signs makes me feel grateful for them as it gives me a sense of peace that my loved ones are checking in on me.

If you happen to believe, I hope you can find comfort in these signs and messages from your angels as I do mine. My Mom's unwavering love and hard-learned wisdom helped me through life's challenges and continue to do so through her signs and my blessed message, but most of all, it shows me how selfless pure love can be...even from a whispered message from heaven.

"If one day the moon calls you by your name don't be surprised,
because every night I tell her about you."

Shahrazad al-Khalij

LINDA S NELSON

"Let your heart guide you...
it whispers so listen closely." - Walt Disney

When Whispers Become Roars: A Journey of Heart and Soul

It started with a whisper – as it has so many times in my life. The question for me was (and always is!) – am I listening?

More times than I can count, I must experience a "forced pause," resulting in a time of reflection to pay attention because those whispers are hard to hear through the noise and distractions of life.

My most recent forced pause was some challenging issues with my physical heart. My heart was whispering to me that there was a problem. I was experiencing fatigue, brain fog and lack of energy and concentration. I had some occurrence of blurred vision, more than normal frequent hiccups and some barely noticeable heart palpitations.

Those whispers grew louder as my heart struggled to beat efficiently. Finally – it got my attention to the point I HAD to listen to those whispers. I experienced extreme fatigue – no energy or motivation to do much of anything. I couldn't concentrate and it felt like my extremities couldn't go on. It was as if the blood wasn't getting to my legs. And I was so short of breath I couldn't go to the mailbox or take a shower or clean the house without having to sit down and catch my breath. Over time, it started to impact my mind, soul and body.

After a long journey of being diagnosed with persistent Afib – a health challenge with the heart that causes my heart to beat inefficiently with high heart rate and being out of rhythm. In my case – more than six months of being out of rhythm 90% more than in rhythm. And a heart that raced – even when I was sitting. My body was screaming – "pay attention to the whispers."

After an unsuccessful series of electro cardio versions, several drug changes, an ablation, a five-day monitoring of my heart in the heart for a risky drug – it has now finally been in rhythm for a record 17 consecutive days as of this writing! I am grateful that I listened to the whispers before they roared. It was truly a transformative experience.

I have learned many lessons during this time of forced pause. Health is something I have taken for granted in my life. You would think that at almost 75 years of age– I would have increased my wisdom of this over the years! Maybe you can relate. Why is it that I need a "wake up" call to pay closer attention to my choices?

I am learning that those whispers – if we listen – are important indicators of our overall health. I am learning the extreme interconnectedness of our mind, body and soul. And how uniquely we are created even though we may all have the same parts. We are still unique in how they work together. I have learned to lean into my faith – that God will work it all out for good. That is His character. And He proves it time after time to me. IF I only pay attention to those "whispers." I am learning that God is up to something during these "forced pauses" to get me to pay attention. He is preparing me for what is to come. And these lessons He teaches me – IF I listen to the "whispers" will be used for His good for me – and for those in my circle of influence.

During this time, I tried to remain positive and look at the benefits of cementing these lessons in my mind too. I had to take better care of myself. Bad habits creep in so subtlety and so fast – I often didn't realize how far off track I had become. I found myself doubting if I was doing the right things for optimum health. So many thoughts were racing through my mind.

Was I drinking enough water? Was I drinking too much caffeine? Was I consuming too much sugar and salt due to not reading labels closely enough? Was I getting enough quality sleep? Was I intentional enough with my mind too? Spending time with my devotion and quiet time? Was I listening to God as He tried to direct my steps? Was I taking the much-needed time to reflect and note what I was learning? The good news? All these questions racing through my mind were lessons He was trying to teach me when I paused to listen.

I have learned through this process how important it is to pay attention to those whispers – not only the physical ones. I am learning to listen to those quiet whispers of God's trying to speak to my soul as well.

You see, God lives in our hearts. That's the sacred place where the Holy Spirit lives deep within us. That is where discernment – and intuition live. But God isn't one to force His will on us. He just asks that 'we come away with Him." Escape with Him from the noise and distractions of the world. Get in touch with Him through silence – and solitude. That is where we'll find answers to our questions – where those whispers can make a difference in the future actions, we take toward the life He wants for us. And those answers give us peace for the challenges we face.

Ultimately, the greatest lesson I learned is the importance of loving yourself as much as God does. Self-care always seemed to me to be selfish practice. Especially when so many in my life require my focus on them.

February is love month – and interestingly it is also heart awareness month. I love that! It's a reminder that I need to love myself enough to care for me – to make me a priority. Because that ultimately benefits all those who count on me to be my best self. It allows me to serve out of abundance of love – starting with myself and spilling over to others.

How about you? Are there whispers that you've been ignoring in the busyness and noise of your life? Are you taking time for you? Are you loving yourself enough to make you a priority?

Don't wait until those whispers turn into a roar you can no longer ignore. Commit to love yourself as God does from this moment forward!

"I was smiling yesterday,
I am smiling today and I will smile tomorrow.
Simply because life is too short to cry for anything."

Santosh Kalwar

CALLI JENSEN

"Have enough courage to trust love one more time and always one more time." - Maya Angelou

True Love Starts From Within. The Rising of the Phoenix.

This story is dedicated to the love of my life, D.

My name is Calli Jensen. My story starts with learning to love again, learning to love myself. Focusing on healing my past trauma has allowed me to attract my soulmate. After years of abuse and broken relationships, there was something that was the common denominator. It was me!

Over the years, I went through some major abuse and heartbreak, being cheated on multiple times in many relationships. I was broken inside. I was unlovable. I had zero hopes.

It wasn't until I started loving myself, I was able to give myself to someone else. I never thought I would ever find true love and attract my perfect match. This was impossible until I realized I needed to learn to love myself again.

It was on my 40th birthday when everything changed for me. I was asked to pose nude and be body painted for a magazine. I was so scared I canceled three times. I was worried about what everyone else would think, how it would come across in my business relationships, my mother's opinion of me, and what everyone would say.

I cannot count how many times I have looked in the mirror and tried to see what was wrong with me. I judged my body constantly and asked myself, "Why was I not good enough?"

Why would I always be hurt and cheated and worse? Constantly lied to, and I was never good enough for anyone else? I was a pawn in their games, and they were always looking for something better.

I was unlovable and broken inside. It felt like my heart was cold as ice even resorted to drugs and alcohol to numb myself. Until the day I did the magazine photoshoot. That was the day my love for myself changed.

Being painted nude was something I had never imagined doing. Let alone being painted by a man! When I arrived, they assured me things would be okay. My good friend Laura Lee calmed me down while doing my hair and makeup. Today, I am forever grateful for her 🖤

Once we were done with hair and makeup, it was my turn to be painted nude from head to toe! The nerves were starting up again, but they were playing some empowering music, which really helped!

When Alix started to paint me, I felt a rush of pain leave my body with every single paint stroke. It was giving me goosebumps as if it was wiping my trauma away with each stroke. It was such an empowering feeling. Being painted for four hours, they chose a Phoenix rising from the flames to paint my entire body! The theme was very fitting at the time. I was coming out of a long relationship. I just started a new business called Our Beauty Referral Network. I was taking control of my life and health.

During the photo shoot, I even cried a little. I felt a huge release of pain, trauma, abuse, and fear. And most of all, in that moment, I learned to accept myself and all my flaws.

I learned to love myself for the first time in my entire life. It was the first time I looked at my body naked in a mirror and loved what I saw. I smiled at my nude-painted body and did not care what anyone else thought. The constant feeling of not being good enough went away with each brush stroke. To this day, I am forever grateful to Laura Lee and Alix for allowing me to accept myself and love myself and my body again.

All the emotions I had coming into this were slowly going away, and I was standing, looking at myself in a mirror once we were done. I had a new image of my body, a new love and appreciation for me again.

Dealing with severe abuse, cervical cancer, and lumps in my breasts and going for multiple tests really messes with your mental health. On top of being sterilized from the covid vax really took a toll on my mental health. My biggest dream is to become a mom and give my mother, Judi, a grandchild to love.

I have had to become my own health advocate and try to figure out why I was so sick. The vax stopped my period and put me into early menopause with zero warning. It caused some severe issues in my health, energy, and hormones. I fought with my doctor for years, and she kept telling me my blood work was normal. I refused to listen to her when I was only 39!! I went for multiple tests, live blood analysis, hormone testing, ultrasound on my uterus, and to a naturopath.

Healing my trauma and focusing on my mindset have been one of the best things I could have done for myself. During one of the most difficult times of my life. After numerous issues with my health and doing everything in my power to figure out what was wrong with me. My goal has always been to fall in love and have my family. Two and a half years ago, I was able to reconnect with the most amazing man in the world.

Back story..... We met on my 21st birthday while on a girl's trip in Seattle and had been friends for 20+ years. A few summers ago, I drove myself and got all my stuff in Toronto, which had been in storage since COVID. During that drive, we spoke and video chatted the entire time and got to truly know each other in a way that was incredible. I am so grateful for him every single day!! D supports me in every way possible. We have everything in common. He is an entrepreneur who loves the outdoors, camping, fishing, and music; he loves to dance and travel. This man is my soulmate.

I never imagined having a love like this. He has been my rock throughout all of the health issues. He wants to give me the gift of becoming a mom. Attracting my soulmate and love of my life has been such a blessing. I never would have imagined that one of my closest friends, after reconnecting, would turn out to be the person I want to spend forever with!

It shows that when you heal yourself you can attract the person who loves you unconditionally. The funny part is he was right there the whole time! He met me when I was WILD, to say the least, and I definitely was not marriage material in my 20s. I admit to being a wild child and out of control. I am grateful every day for all the experiences, growth, and healing that I have gone through in the past 10 years.

They say you can not change the past, but you have a choice about how your future plays out. I strongly believe and have faith in everything I am currently creating in my life. All of the health issues and trauma, as well as healing myself, have allowed me to create the most magical relationships.

It has also given me the experiences in life to create Our Beauty Referral Network and use this business to support the community through their health and wellness journey. Our company allows customers and businesses to earn an income working from home while healing themselves through all our amazing partnerships with natural practitioners and wellness partners.

My vision is coming to life to connect humanity on a deeper level, form lasting relationships, and heal the world.

"Sometimes I wonder if there's something wrong with me. Perhaps I've spent too long in the company of my literary romantic heroes, and consequently, my ideals and expectations are far too high."

E.L. James

ANGELA RUNQUIST

"Mountaintops are for views and inspiration,
but fruit is grown in the valleys." - Billy Graham

A Story of Love, Hope, and a Cord of Three Strands

When I think of whispers of my heart, I think of communication with God. I believe God listens to the whispers of our hearts even when we don't think our dreams are possible and we seem to have lost all hope.

I had buried the desires of my heart.

After a few bad relationships, ending in divorce, I had decided it was better for me to be alone. I didn't want to take the chance on being hurt... again. I had built up walls of protection and had no plans to get emotionally tied to a man again.

God had other plans for my life. He heard the silent whispers of my heart that I didn't want to acknowledge. I am now engaged to a wonderful man and planning our wedding in a few months. Our story began five years ago.

We first met at my place of employment where David was a client. We gradually became friends and remained casual friends for the next few years. I moved on to another job and eventually I sold my house and moved to another state seven hours away.

Almost two years ago, I went back to visit friends and family. David and I reconnected over a cup of coffee and a drive. We talked for a couple of hours and then, once again, went our separate ways. I was determined to keep my walls of protection strongly in place.

David started sending me text messages occasionally and we continued to communicate through text for several months. He was always a gentleman and never pushed for more than friendship, which was still all I was willing to give. Then the day came when David decided to be straight forward and honest about his intentions. Looking back on it now, I would also say he was pretty brave as well.

David told me that he had been praying for someone to share his life with. He told me that he thought I was "a beautiful woman that could be marriage material". I received that message from him at the same time I was having what I thought was a gallbladder attack. I told him I would have to talk to him later and left him hanging.

I spent six hours in the emergency room that night only to hear they couldn't find anything wrong. I decided it must have been bad sausage on a pizza earlier that day.

After a few days I finally responded to David's message about marriage. I had needed some time to collect my thoughts. When I finally responded, I told him that nothing had changed, and I still could only offer him friendship. I said that just thinking about anything more than that caused fear and anxiety, that I had major relationship PTSD and trust issues. I went on to tell him that I'm broken and after all I have been through, anyone who wants to be a part of my life needs to understand that, be honest, completely transparent and have a lot of patience. David's response was "yes, mam,

God bless" and then asked how I was feeling after my emergency room visit. I was sure my response to his message about marriage would scare him away.

Instead, David continued to send text messages asking about my day and praying that God would bless our walk with Him. Most of our messages consisted of saying good morning and have a great day. We had not had more than a couple actual phone conversations. Thinking back on that, I think it was a subconscious way of continuing to protect my heart. If we had real conversations, it would be taking a risk of getting too close.

He then started sending me pictures of the daily devotional he was reading along with his good morning messages. After consistently receiving the daily devotions, the walls of my heart started to crack a bit. David asked me one day if I would do a devotion with him on a Bible app titled God Heals. When you do one of these Bible app devotions with someone else it gives you and the other person an opportunity to share your thoughts after doing the reading.

Our communication by text became more than just good morning messages and would include what was going on in our day to day lives. We started having actual phone conversations and began to talk about our families and our past relationships. About heartache, addiction and abuse.

That soon changed to talking about hope and the possibility of a future. Jeremiah 29:11 NKJV says "For I know the thoughts that I think toward you, says the Lord, thoughts of peace and not of evil, to give you a future and a hope."

The more we shared through doing devotions together, long conversations on the phone and our short, in person visits, those whispers of the heart began to seep through the cracks and dissolve that wall I had spent years building and making sure was strong and unbreakable. This made me a tad bit nervous but instead of running the other direction, I invited David to be my plus one at my family Thanksgiving.

Until we walked in together at Thanksgiving dinner, I had kept our growing relationship quiet. Surprisingly it went well, and my family welcomed him in. After our time together Thanksgiving weekend I couldn't stop thinking about him. A few days later I was listening to a few songs on YouTube and the song, My Heart is Open by Keith Urban came on. I listened to that song a few times and realized it was true. My heart was open. Open to new love and the hope of a better future. My walls had definitely come crashing down.

I sent David that song. He responded, letting me know he understood my message and was very thankful. He then told me that he had been praying for this; that I would be able to open my heart to him. We have developed a strong love for each other, but we also know that, to have a successful marriage, we need the wisdom to know how to build the foundation of our relationship and coming marriage.

Ecclesiastes 4:12 says, "a cord of three strands is not quickly broken". That cord of three strands is David, me and Jesus.

To gain the wisdom needed for this strong foundation we are going through another devotion together on the Bible app on marriage, reading a book together on choosing God's best and have begun premarital counseling.

I am so thankful that I listened to those quiet whispers of the heart and look forward to our future filled with love and wisdom.

"The greatest happiness of life is the conviction that we are loved; loved for ourselves, or rather, loved in spite of ourselves."

Victor Hugo

PART 2

ABOUT WOMEN LIKE ME

"Love has nothing to do with what you are expecting to get–only with what you are expecting to give–which is everything."

Katharine Hepburn

THE WOMEN LIKE ME COMMUNITY

A PLACE TO BELONG, A SPACE TO WRITE, A MOVEMENT TO INSPIRE

If you're not already part of the **Women Like Me Community**, I invite you to step into a space where women come together to uplift, empower, and share their voices. This is more than just a social network—it's a **writing community** filled with women who have stories to tell, wisdom to share, and dreams to bring to life.

Here, you'll find connection, encouragement, and inspiration from like-minded women who understand the journey of life, the power of words, and the importance of lifting each other up. Whether you're a seasoned writer, a first-time author, or someone who simply wants to share your truth, this is a place where your words matter.

Throughout the year, we collaborate on **Women Like Me Community books**, like the one you are reading now. Every woman in our community is invited to contribute, and there's **no cost to participate**—just a willingness to share your story and inspire others. If you've ever dreamed of becoming a published author, this is your chance to take that first step in a supportive and welcoming environment.

More than just a writing group, the **Women Like Me Community** is a movement. Whether you're a working professional, an entrepreneur, or a stay-at-home mom, you'll find **mentors, role models, and friendships** that will help you grow—not just as a writer, but as a woman embracing her full potential.

If you've been searching for a place where you can be **seen, heard, and valued**, this is it.

Your story matters. Your voice matters. **You matter.**

Don't wait—join us today and start writing the next chapter of your life!

Women Like Me Community – Julie Fairhurst https://www.facebook.com/groups/879482909307802

"In love there are two things– bodies and words."

Joyce Carol Oates

THE WOMEN LIKE ME BOOK SERIES

Everyone has a story. And oftentimes, those stories can be powerful things that help us learn and grow. But for some people, their stories can be a source of pain. They may feel like they can't escape their past or that their story is holding them back from living their best lives.

If you're one of those people, know that you're not alone. And more importantly, know that there is hope. There are ways to turn your personal story into something positive and to find healing from the past.

One way is to share your story with others. This can be incredibly cathartic, and it can also help others who have been through similar experiences. You process your feelings and work through any trauma you may be carrying around.

And finally, don't forget that your story doesn't define you. You are more than your history. You are more than your pain. You are more than your mistakes. You are more than your story. You are strong, you are brave, and you are enough. So don't let your story hold you back.

Writing about your past can be very beneficial, both emotionally and psychologically. You can increase your feelings of well-being and even improve your physical health. When you write about your past experiences, you relive them in your mind. This can help you to process difficult or traumatic events, and it can also provide you with some closure.

Additionally, writing about your past can help you better understand yourself and work through any unresolved issues. It can also allow you to see yourself in a new light, which can be both healing and empowering. In addition to helping you emotionally, writing about your past can also be beneficial physically.

Studies have shown that expressive writing can help to reduce stress, anxiety, and depression. It can also help to improve your immune system function and promote a sense of calm. So, if you're feeling stressed or overwhelmed, consider picking up a pen and starting to write.

We only have one shot at this life, and it's our only shot. There are no do-overs. There are no second chances. So, we better make the most of it. We only have this moment right here, right now, and it's the only moment that matters. We are only given so much time on this planet and must spend it wisely. We only have so much energy and want to spend it on things that bring us joy. We only have so much love and want to give it to people who appreciate it.

If you're a woman with life experiences, the world wants to hear from you. Visit my website at www.juliefairhurst.com and get in touch. The world will be waiting.

A story is powerful. It can draw you in, take you on a journey, and leave you lasting impressions. That's why I love listening to other people's stories. Everyone has a story, and I'm always eager to hear a new one.

I want to hear from you. You can reach me by visiting my website and letting me know you're ready to tell your story. The world is waiting to hear what you have to say. So, what are you waiting for?

Get in touch today!

Women Like Me Stories https://womenlikemestories.com/tell-your-story/

"Love makes your soul crawl out from its hiding place."

Zora Neale Hurston

MORE FROM WOMEN LIKE ME

Books are available on Amazon or the Women Like Me Stories website. If you can't find the book you are looking for, contact me, and I can help. Or if you would like an autographed copy, please email at julie@changeyourpath.ca

---

Women Like Me Book Series

This is a collection in which women open their hearts, sharing chapters of their lives to inspire and guide others on their journey through life.

- Women Like Me – A Celebration of Courage and Triumphs
- Women Like Me – Stories of Resilience and Courage
- Women Like Me – A Tribute to the Brave and Wise
- Women Like Me – Breaking Through the Silence
- Women Like Me – From Loss to Living
- Women Like Me – Healing and Acceptance
- Women Like Me – Reclaiming Our Power
- Women Like Me – Whispers of Warriors: Women Who Refused to Stay Broken
- Women Like Me – Embracing the Unseen – The Courage to Surrender
- Women Like Me - Transforming Pain Into Wisdom and Love
- Women Like Me - When Life Breaks You Open - Moments That Change Everything

---

Women Like Me Community Book Series

The community books are a testament to the power of our beautiful members from all around the world. These remarkable women share their thoughts, experiences, and wisdom, creating books of inspiration and guidance for all.

- Women Like Me Community – Messages to My Younger Self
- Women Like Me Community – Sharing Words of Gratitude
- Women Like Me Community – Sharing What We Know to Be True
- Women Like Me Community – Journal for Self-Discovery
- Women Like Me Community – Sharing Life's Important Lessons
- Women Like Me Community – Having Better Relationships
- Women Like Me Community – Honoring the Women in Our Lives
- Women Like Me Community – Letters to Our Future Selves
- Women Like Me Community – The Warrior Within
- Women Like Me Community – Whisper's Within the Power of Women's Intuition
- Women Like Me Community – Dreams That Speak the Power Of Women's Dreams
- Women Like Me Community – Graceful Guidance Treasured Advice and Love From One Generation to The Next
- Women Like Me Community – Whispers of the Heart True Stories of Love and Wisdom

---

Women Like Me in Kenya

100% of the profits go directly to these 26 Kenyan Authors. The Women Like Me Program covers all costs of producing and publishing Kenyan books.

These women are mostly widowed and live in extreme poverty. They use the proceeds to pay school fees so their children can get an education. No school fees mean children

cannot go to school. They also purchase food and clothing for their children.

If you would like to support these amazing women in Kenya, please reach out to Julie at julie@changeyourpath.ca

- Women Like Me – Strong Women in Kenya
- Women Like Me – Through the Eyes of Kenyan Women
- Women Like Me – The Children of Kenya

Sales and Personal Growth

Julie Fairhurst offers a wealth of knowledge through her books on achieving success in business and life. With a remarkable 34-year career as an entrepreneur, her expertise spans sales, marketing, promotion, and writing.

www.juliefairhurst.com

- The Julie Fairhurst Story – Healing Generations, One Story at a Time
- From Idea to Bestseller – Writing for Self-Help Authors
- Positivity Makes All the Difference
- Powerful Persuasion – Unlocking the Five Key Strategies for Business Success
- Transferring Enthusiasm - The Sales Book for Your Business Growth
- Agent Matchmaker: How to Find Your Real Estate Soulmate"
- Agent Etiquette – 14 Things You Didn't Learn in Real Estate School
- 7 Keys to Success – How to Become a Real Estate Badass
- 30 Days to Real Estate Action – Real Strategies & Real Connections
- Why Agents Quit the Business

"Nobody has ever measured, even poets, how much a heart can hold."

Zelda Fitzgerald

JULIE FAIRHURST

EMPOWERING WOMEN THROUGH STORYTELLING AND INFLUENCE

Julie Fairhurst is the visionary **Founder of the Women Like Me Book Program**, a groundbreaking initiative that has empowered over **160 women to become published authors**. With **300+ true-life stories published** and **over 30 books released**, many of which have achieved **#1 Best Seller status**, Julie has created a platform where women can share their voices, inspire others, and leave a lasting legacy.

What sets the **Women Like Me Book Program** apart is its commitment to accessibility and empowerment. Some women in the program are given the opportunity to **become published authors at no cost**, ensuring that every woman, regardless of financial circumstances, has the chance to share her truth with the world.

Beyond publishing, Julie is a **renowned speaker, trainer, and educator** with **34 years of expertise in sales and marketing**. A **Master Persuader** with deep insights into human behavior, she specializes in helping **women entrepreneurs** build **influence, establish authority, and increase revenue** through powerful storytelling, strategic marketing, and high-impact sales techniques.

Julie's personal journey—marked by **overcoming adversity, loss, and hardship**—has fueled her passion for **mentoring women**, guiding them to **rise above their challenges, own their stories, and embrace their fullest potential**.

Whether through her books, coaching, or speaking engagements, Julie's mission is clear: **to inspire, uplift, and transform lives—one story at a time.**

Manufactured by Amazon.ca
Acheson, AB